IN THE HEART
OR OUR CITY

Random House

NEW YORK

RAPHAEL RUDNIK
IN THE HEART
OR OUR CITY

Library of Congress Cataloging in Publication Data

Rudnik, Raphael.   In the heart or our city.
Poetry.
I. Title.
PS3568.U3515   811'.5'4   72-8383
ISBN 0-394-48064-3 (hardbound)
ISBN 0-394-70618-8 (paperbound)

The following poems originally appeared in:
Counter/Measures:
"For a Young Girl"
The Humanist:
"Night-Pieces"
The Nation:
"Talking to the Sky"
Open Places:
"Dots and Dashes"
"Bright Fall"
"A Message from the Dawn"
"Jewels of Arabia"
The Quarterly Review of Literature:
"The End of a Day"
"This Story of Troy"
"Aria"
"Elements of Immortality"
"Broken Ballad" was first published in *Poetry*, February 1973. Copyright © 1973 by Modern Poetry Association.
Type set by Cherry Hill Composition, Pennsauken, N.J.
Manufactured in the United States of America
Printed and Bound by Kingsport Press,
Kingsport, Tenn.
First Edition

acknowledgment

With grateful thanks to the John Simon
Guggenheim Memorial Foundation, for
the assistance and honor of their Fellow-
ship.

for MARYKA

CONTENTS

I

TALKING TO THE SKY

II
IN THE HEART OR OUR CITY

I

TALKING TO
THE SKY

Broken Ballad

The dock is gay with streamers, but the boat
Has not come or gone, never will be built.
On scum-laden water, crazy rainbows split.
Take it from me there's less to this than that.

An angel-headed dandelion has got
To break in wind, whenever the wind blows
The thing will fly in more ways than it knows.
Take it from me there's less to this than that.

There is a blue flower, on a hill hot
With yellow sunlight, below a black and white
Cathedral stained by immaculate light.
Take it from me there's less to this than that.

The brackish, feverish taste was not
Good, in that first kiss—far, deep from us, lips
Wandered, murmuring sibilants . . . *polyps.*
Take it from me there's less to this than that.

See, crystaled green tattering celebrate—
Presences of impersonal rage! Trees move
In slow, thoughtless insignias of our love . . .
Take it from me there's less to this than that.

A drunkard staggered rubber-legged, fell flat
In front of me. As I picked him up,
He screamed: *"Pick me up you bastard, pick me up!"*
Take it from me there's less to this than that.

No squad of strolling lovers has the state
Of blood-red roses—nor do they need hearts
To be true, like our anatomy-charts.
Take it from me there's more to this than that.

Your thighs, made of marvelous stuff—that
Bright, intrusive silk moving in deep light.
I wanted to touch until I touched that light.
Take it from me there's more to this than that.

Your body. A gold and white island. It
Was more naked than the skeleton
Of God. It seemed you were the only one.
Take it from me there's more to this than that.

You laughed at a clock, figuring us out:
"The hands move, hold nothing—yet, once or twice
Joy turned them back." The face was blank as ice.
Take it from me there's more to this than that.

Where did you get that deathless look set
Like what Marvell called glancing wheels that kill
Into my gaze before I looked my full?
Take it from me there's more to this than that.

There's more to this than that, or you or me,
For trees and boats are clocks, and flowers fall
In ways that drunkards do—through the light, *all*—
Cathedraling rainbows, broken like sea.

Dirge

Color and wind of the season,
Close down to the hollow tomb.
The dark alone breathes reason
Where saddened spirits come.

Though he was shy and gentle,
Regret is vain and numb.
Clamorous clouds like metal
Shields hover near the tomb.

The lonely, slow brightness
He held to in his time
Is only on the surface.
Below, the startling tomb.

Talking to the Sky

Until this day, his eyes had the tender and thoughtless blue of the sky. Now they looked like, and at, sky running with grey fingers, fumbling past the shabby coin of light.

A bee big as a thumb buzzed, a blood-colored bird flew up the hill, a bell sounded out its iron tremor (if it could speak would it summon God not man?), the white hearts of the grass were about to depart from the ground—he stood and spoke to the sky.

"Gigantic meat-safe—angels going by in ones and twos . . . past that bloody, oversized comma, cut out of her golden body gone grey—wings a little too white and new!"

Up, up from her little brown house bulging on the hill stuttered smoke; wincing and blowing away like his sentence.

"I did not know, how strong you are—" Then the grey opening a metal yellow flower (whose fiery particles outlive each thing and moment, offering power?) like her eyes when she told him it had been done.

No child. Never even got to be the bubblehead and body mapped by veins floating in her hunched prayerfully, waiting (to unvoice the reeling darkness of chance?) to cry in the nothing of air.

"I am real. I am I. I hate you. She—" He saw her desperate in a garden somewhere (where?) with a child, carrying a cat cradled in a shoe-box coffin, stomach open, maimed, meteorlike eyes—(interested in something?) (Why is it he thought of a hawk batting down from the monstrous, inap-

propriate height of sky in lost, fierce pride?)

Rain fell—slapping like flesh on flesh, stopped. Scared away (by what kind hand brought alive to a strange place?) a shimmering, yellow-green lizard.

Up—up—from the ground came the head—hair slowly waving like the grass in wind—a mortal shine (insane, compassionate smile?) on its face.

Thinking of God, he tamed his face. Then it turned into a stone.

"Years, years—" he cried out to the stone.

Then it was gone.

Darker and darker grew the valley, more and more forgetting. The bright growth day died.

Wordlessly he spoke her, wordlessly. Till sound cried and failed near stars, as tall trees pointed like instruments at a white membrane of moon.

Some Birds for Mooka

Two birds suddenly out of nowhere locked together twittering go up like one climbing a mirror then fall flying apart.

*

Dans ces mêmes régions la perdrix rouge procure de fortes émotions au chasseur endurant et experimenté.

The dogs (starved lean in cellars all winter for sinister accomplishment, and to look good with guns and masters) cry out—in a voice more human than the one from wine-rouged faces: *"Did not your great- and great-great- to the greatest grand-father do it ... and your father?"*

History as The Society of Hereditary Legislators, eager to snap life open and shut. There, there—that was a—*bang!*

What are people to do, sit watching insects in the ugly little town of a rotting bee—the slow, soundless artillery of the mist advancing—time? *Bang!*

*

A body full of white circles outlined by black, like the shine and dark reflex of stars, earth-colored underneath, broken by beating wings, face tipped into the sky, little red legs standing in air—*lifteth.*

*

His triple-nippled red top flops up and down, or lies flat like an old cardinal hat. The gold-crusted blue-dark cloak works, with the stalking strut.

His three brown hens (and a new soft glow, like light on hair of girls not quite women) retreat in a willing-waddle.

9

Squawking vexes, pecking plushbottoms—he moves their moving, beyond possessiveness.

*

Propped in a house of straw,
A tattered flower sleeping.
A bee in the field alone,
Finds nothing for safekeeping.
Smoke like a crystal hung,
Dispersed, a cloud of violence—
The hunter broke his silence . . .

The bee is becoming mad.
The flower still is sleeping.
The old, hungry sun sinks down.
The frowning hunter leaping
To see, to see what he has done!
Bright sticks of straw grow dark.
Vague, wet—broken wings? No mark.

The sound of the shot is gone.
The bee, a pilotless drone.
The field seems almost not there.
The flower buried in air.
Brightening O of the moon,
Where is the wounded one—
Soul, undoing and undone?

A Message from the Dawn

Light-alive grey broken, centered by red.
Red in a huge cone was spreading on the waves;

Waves rising over falling down. The forms
Forms of each other—breaking sky-hollow, light.

Bright Fall

The wrecking-ball sun seems to start itself into a broad-backed, heltering kite that splits with light. Red streamers like blood refusing to fall.

Then brightness falls from its source in taut, stuttering scythe-swing arcs.

The End of a Day

Trees going yes and no and something circular in-between in wind. Pale flags in dark wood frost snapped riding into the deepening conclusion of light.

Jewels of Arabia

Empty branches beneath the blind crux of stars.

The orange-faced listener shakes his fire, sending sparks in an arc, laughs icy breaths: *"Jewels of Arabia."*

Poet in the Valley

On a piece of paper glowing among broken letters of twigs (punctuated by ant-holes) stone silences and whispering grass:

HERMAN THE ANT

Here he comes, carrying a crust—like a man with a sail through thickest jungle. Slips down a bent grass spire, hangs by his mouth from the caught crust—tininesses treading air—falls. Down, marches on, his own emblem and treasure, of food and work. The unimpeded servant of dignified (because the *fact,* of his current of life) misery. Crosses the moonous, mirroring stair (stare) of a trail left by a snail. Above centuries of bones, below warm mouths pulling grass from the planet, he—

In the hand of the poet now, the page billowed, dancing like a big white flower—its cheeks puffed out.

is aware . . . of the big, beaded ant-body of his queen (in heights evolved, a cathedral); and the abacus of his friends, the ordinary ones he worked with around the hole. That strange little core of emptiness. Alive with something stronger than strength—the element of undivided trust—work.

Something legendary in those smallest particulars, but not song. He let the page go—a map of mist, into the mist.

*

15

It was late. He still had not found the few lines he needed each day, to polish the lustrous knife and fork of his sanity.

Look at the flowers. Bronze suede of marigolds, one he had not seen before on a broken stalk, grown past its own support ("Like any vanity!") and the red rose.

They did not sing to him, but he said: "I am the poet in the valley" with pride, then cheerfulness—"And you are the valley!"

*

The field was thick with spirits.

Blue-grey rocks, fallen fruit of the crag (each a ruined city) possessed the empty grass. Further, bow-legged trees leaned together like old men (like him) out for a walk. Black arrows of birds shot between them. And further, a hundred or so helmet-headed clumps, in rows . . . around a young white tree leaning forward under disheveled leaves. Towering over them with unreal life—funny, but sad— because the perfection of their unranked order was so abstract.

Walking near the house (where an orange-lighted lamp was reading itself over a bed of straw sleeping on straw, and a flower of smoke stuck in the chimney) a shine stabbing the ground. A black shape, of sleep or sickness, rose, led the light away so fast it lost it. "Carrying its shadow to hell" the poet wrote, as if he could tell . . .

That little bread he had hid near the white tree—the dawn-meal for the mouse . . .

*

The field twisted—dwindling, disappearing into itself. Leaves uplifted like fright-wigs in the line of trees.

The hollow, glotal yodeling knock of goat-bells.

A man in blue, a shepherd! Brown dog yipping, bouncing

around, looping in soft, disconnected leaps—sheep running on their own shadows on grass like cracking green glass.

What complicated, glowing squalor, a farm! And a golden crucible of hay in the light, red combs of a cock perched upon,—pouring silver sound into dawn rinsing down all the invisible grey eyes of the sky like blood down broken glass.

The house wider, wider, slanting down to the field. Crumbling stone stumbling to the ground, revealing wizened beams. White little goats run out, white beards, white eyes . . . A wingless model airplane nailed on a post, enamel-slick green body glistening, propeller turning, humming in the wind . . .

The house threw down its stones. And when the place was almost dead, a young woman with honey-colored hair and a smile of startled shyness came out. (The smile reflects . . . a big hill and a far field, a house-top cut away by time—what a big room laid bare, bigger than . . . what? Fires of flowers around thick, grey stone edges. It slopes down.) And see, the blue shepherd! He digs a hole with his long stick, face aglow. The honey-lady spills toward it . . . the sun sinks down dulled, like brown steel-studded leather!

Hills block the horizon, jagged folds—sun breaks them open—mindless strays of sunlight breaking into flowers, plants, birds, and bad creatures.

The insides of his eyelids, heavy and closed—opened. All around, married by the immensity of moonlit night—hill-mountains marched. A cloud had come down to rest on the highest one.

"Are the great buried alive in the sky?" the poet asked, in his book.

In front of him—a wine-stain purple and green starfish-shaped plant, one drop of mist and moonlight on it, magnifying bronzed, whorling dust, or decay.

*

How much he was, in fact—each thing in the valley!

At first, he demanded to know of things—what justice the soul could expect, coupled to a singing intellect for life. Monsters of originality formed on the field, on his page. Then, one day—he witnessed and defended the creation of his whole life.

Steel spirits shot through the wooden hill! Smoking black bars held by men moved like a broken prison through the vague, mordant flank of the hill.

They were gone so fast, he knew nothing was dead.

A sleep and bread later, he found the place.

A sudden gathering of goodness!—Joy was mountainous, making everything in the valley in him, rising toward it.

*

Some sullen fish why was the world dead with a black pool packed in a gold ring rinsed with blood (eye) stuffed in his mouth a shrimp like a pipe (in the market in the morning the sky leaned up hills hunched together as he slanted down to the town) the cricket-faced dog saw him pass—cheeses colored coins of some giant kingdom, swollen bronze coins rusted seagreen suddenly rock walls closing in on the road sounds playing big but still absence of echo

That was enough of that.

*

Moonspangled mist, rolled around the bright heads of the flowers—like an idiot among his baubles.

18

The kindly, queer and unafraid
Are straightened out and they are made
Like me, like me . . .

Ah!

What else could they want to be?
Whatever human fault remains
Is screened out by the gauze of veins . . .

The poet writes quickly, as the mist sings to him on a
sudden, moving depth of wind:

A smooth cold cloth will set you right
And let you sleep both day and night
Like me, like me . . .

And:

And when the sheer uncrusted paint
Covers you up without a point
Like me, like me . . .
There's no one else you'll want to be!

He writes after the little song: "The mist is a traveler of
unknown origin, and its own destination."
"*To be, to be . . .*" the wind echoes.

*

His eyes are shut like his book—in the bloody glow of the light. He lies down on the straw, trying not to see the tattered flowers there. He reaches up, and lifts the orange latch of light into darkness.

He dreams, of the sun. The red god of his poetic destiny —awaits.

This Story of Troy

"Something more must be done with this story of Troy" said the Director. "Let's have death as a young lady in leather skirts pulling in the horse, and let's make the horse real with eyes for no one but the girl. That's great, she'll emerge as a symbol as the men emerge from the horse—they've been swallowed in a flashback—But, until then, she'll only be a dumb broad doing her job well . . . she wants to be the first woman jockey in the city of the Gods. They have a circle around that imaginary city where horses always race. Mounted by passion that never falls through lack of love or pain or pity. Horses in that imaginary city race round at their own intervals, mounted by passion that never falls through lack of love, or pain or pity. Horses in that—"

Aria

The fat, black-clad doughy whorl sitting either sleeping or weeping. The bold, bald little musclebound tenor follows his golden, blasting voice onstage singing his ships are in the harbor pointing their tall masts at the moon and he comes for her. He fingers a moonbeam—near her now; then gives a genuflecting bow.

Her eyes open looks of unrequited self-love, as she climbs up and down the one word, *thou.*

Dots and Dashes

A poet wants to know the name of rows of little round candy on a paper strip. He phones a candy factory and gets switched around ("Just try anything that goes" says Publicity, "Barbells?" asks the Record Room) by a serious ("Is it 'Dots'?") operator until his question is finally cast at the manufacturer who whispers: "Button-candy."

The poet worries next about punctuation: "Is there that little dash between?" "No dashes—and not 'Dots' . . . *buttons*" the voice comes back quietly, as if in awe of its own temper.

"I mean the thing between, the thing that is always lost in metaphor—the connecting dash, is it there?" "Two words" are the last two words, growled by that guardian of sweet myth, punctuated by a sensual mockery of sucked lips—a dash-destroyer if there ever was one.

Black cords like thick licorice twisted.

Fall-Guy

A red-nosed copper came a-cropper
In a field, looking for cached perfume
Without his scent-senser. He fell through
Into an abandoned copper-mine
Which smelled so bad . . . as if the stopper
Had been pulled from a terrible tomb.

"My nose is working now—it . . . phew!"
He held his breath, then became unclear,
And died. Neither loneliness nor fear
Qualified this lost authority
To know that he would someday die—
Without a criminal near or crime,
Without his hate, or place or time,
Without the way of being moral!

Centaurs

The mettlesome music of hooves.

And then the horses arrived, gliding under slumped smaller animals, stopping then stooping over his broken bottle that reflected the darkening air like a pool.

"See, see they have come," he slurred. *"Sir Linguist with your black book put that in—glassy-eyed centaurs have come without a word to—"*

He tried to get up, but fell from the bench onto the soft, black path, crumpled into sleep—after a rough, uncomprehending look at pages billowing in my black book.

A piece of pus-colored cloud poised like cotton above the needle of a far-off tower.

Villon Hang, High
and Awful As a Sword!

Teeth trying to eat my black tongue,
Neck kicked and raped by my weight—Paris,
Here is my *ha*—prick straight out, stone.

Found guilty of France. I saw the tears
Under blood running down her face;
The bubbles moved slow and were clear.

I fucked Andromache and I fucked her good,
And then all of them cried *alas!*,
Though none of them understood.

Hanging above Paris, I feel the State
In my throat—a kind of dying glass
And shifting gas—deadly, but somewhat late.

And man is a beggar below me,
Scr-r-ratching his ripe ass
In ecstasy. Ah, he finds a flea!

He holds it hard between his nails,
(Dirt-uniformed attendants) and says:
"Bring the court some wine." He smiles his smile.

The other hand does as it is told.
With the solemn, constipated face
Of Justice that has grown too old,

He warns the hidden speck: *"Speak flea, speak—*
A spare and sour face, will not prevent disgrace!"
Then sensing the accused too weak,

Whines, (acting one who has gorged *his* own blood):
"Sire . . . glowing orb, I praise . . . I was
For you, of you—and, growing great and good."

Then comes, the greater voice: "Of *me?* For *me?*
Smug love-creature—(*vade retro Satanas!*)—
I see your innocence, Oh I see—

But, where are *you?* A crime! Deeper than words
(And all their blood-sucking eloquence) as . . .
As bird-shit is deeper than birds!

(How this storm is turning voices, mouth
Into the brain of a beggar that was
Hushed, fetid and still!) "The Truth

Now, are you there?" The hidden pain, silent.
Public dirt and pain answers again: *"Was."*
"Hiding from the court, criminal intent—

The greatest crime is to cost this court time!"
The flea, by now the sorriest fuzz
Between trembling fingers, or a small slime—

Poised at the edge of the death-vat (water,
Not wine) cannot hear the sentence he has.
"Proceed." Faceless, limbless executioners

Rub and slide and scrape against each other.
Till an odd shape of filth rolls in the glass,
Magnified. He drinks it all, (the beggar)

Falls into fever, wants justice above
His own guts—dreaming a golden cutlass;
That cuts the flea out, as he calls it Love!

I scratched and found, and drank my drowned fate,
(Though it had the taste of brass)
To cut love out. The hollow, hanging hate

You see. Not you, pass. Dark night now sings
Full of its will in me. Dies,
Terrible. Not you. Pass. Pity me, nothing.

Elements of Immortality

All along the golden day queens have died young and fair; now—wandering in that beauty-drunken light—Nashe falls.

A sudden flaming word, in clanging space a moment heard, troubling the endless reverie—; the old liar would laugh and bless it from his grave, words are a stony stuff for such as Yeats to save.

Angry, brilliant ocean around Hart Crane now, death's dark horse in motion beats the gargoyled prow.

The courtier Daniel instructs earth, breathes forth new flowers which never yet were known, unto the Spring— and trees, fair branches of power.

Death humiliates Sidney Keyes with its dark, threshing ease. He sought symbolic bird and petal live, in burning gun-metal.

In Hell, Dylan Thomas is carrying beerbarrels overseen by Hitler, a cat on a windowsill, belled. (The poet there part-time, for his blasphemous sophistry: "What is the meter of the dictionary?")

The bright, hard atom on the blind, empty shore of Milton's light inexpressible.

These, and all the dead poets are singing—without help of meter, words or rhyme. Poetry is the sound of love upon the void of time!

For a Young Girl

The moon-sword goes in gold,
Into the black mountain-rim.
And that is what makes you sad,
And this is what makes you lonely:
That badness is always bad—
And goodness goodness only.

Night-Pieces

1.

Outside our door, a tree
Creaking like the
Door it could be.

2.

Stars seem to tinkle and slide
Down into
Cricket-mad night.

3.

Hear—*the gun, love!*
The line of fire in the blood.
The heart, hit.

4.

You will wake all air and rock,
Love—
Stepping from dreams to grass.

The Eagle

The slam of his beating wings
Makes the air that moves him move.
Lonely, alone, lonely
With only the sky to love.

Down a mountain of light,
To the highest hardest place,
Above the edge of deep waters—
He rests. Cloud-giants race.

Hooded eyes scorn the world below,
The great head goes from side to side,
Until force within him, hungry,
Throws him down, and—something has died.

Lost in the Alps

A knight had done everything for his lady, and was to be alone with her for the first time. *"You are a beautiful lady— I've had that thought in my head; you are a beautiful lady, my heart itself has said"*—was the salutation he had prepared, but when he came into the room a bright limbless body and gold head lay faced down on a grey where slow birds, blear-eyed from speed or devouring flew in front of it, clacking. The knight was used to a world of ever-varying visions; but before this his lady had always seemed changing, never unlike herself—she did not kiss or climb (or even show her face) at court, but appeared, as from another place and time . . . like that moon coming through clouds now at the window.

Blinking in the new coherence of light the knight looked down—into cloth (armored yet soft, as an insect) near his knee—a hole! *"Poverty will out!"*—he laughed.

Unraveling threads there showed the story of his love (the manner of world this knight loved was enchantment of the impersonal): a black bent up, banished into indifferent air; a red one stretched out somehow too thin across the hole on his skin; and a gold, afloat upon chill, absenting waters of moonlight. In its golden silver glare still waiting and still watching and still wanting mixed.

Then tenderly touching, widening, unweaving threads, he saw a golden tabernacle whose black blood-stained gate opened onto a lost, innocent track of flesh-colored shapes.

His blood pulsed and whispered like a drum by the sea.

The head and half-body turned, on that greyness like a light-blinded mirror now. A frowning simian smile (as if vice were smiling, when apprehended) on her face. The unseeing gaze (a delta of shadow from the point at each center) of heavy, bright breasts. Below, wide bones in white silk skin grinned aside a cloud of rust-colored hair.

Her hidden mouth, *there*—lips silently working waving like an undersea polyps—unfolding a gold-veined purple embryo of a bird, solemnly nodding its faceless head deep into sublunar sleep—a red stem breaks through, breaks through where flesh is like lizard-skin, a bright blue saddle-patch, gobbet-fingers, a white nub—all contract and grab and change into each other until the fight is over and the victor (who was as men are now) emerging, displayed a gleaming red throat—withdrew, looking brownish-grey.

Her legs walked in the room, alone—so whitely shone. Radial bones of the feet dilating light up into big bright bones at each step set. Swung as one once, crutchlike—were gone. "Obviously, going somewhere—" laughed the knight.

He looked at her, then spoke the words spoken before when, glorious and unreproved—no machine to him, no horse, no squire—he had won her rich kingdoms, special realms, possessions. (Before! The least hutment there still jeweled, surprised his mind like a star.) His oath: "Love, you are an island that lifts into sky when seen."

No-country no-century stars stared at him through the black, backless lot of night—a pale multitude as lost as people lost in the Alps.

He heard their sweet civility, an ardent singing made of love that lived in nothing: *"Deliberate one pass on, pass on—you have no gods until the world is gone!"*

They slipped like smoke through the edifice of his vision.

II

IN THE HEART
OR OUR CITY

In the Heart or Our City

'But what's THAT! Something, somewhere. Where was it?'

'Wind hits, cuts itself on things—grunts, shrieks—outside.'

'It is as if I'd rolled over in the dark
Again, whispering your name, and you still slept.'

'Or, rushing in all those eye-holes up there,
The wind whinnies, stamps and kicks—banging around
The attic more wild horse than ghost. Or—boards creak:
A trick-horse standing on one . . . two three four legs.
Or a sudden, short sharp breath down here can sound
Like a shot out there. So—sleep. Give me your hand.'

'For five nights without fail, the same sounds wake me!
That little, drowned raw bell below our bed.
Then something dragging something above us.'

'There you go dragging in that dragging thing
Again. Listen, this ventriloquial house—'

'—I woke with my heart pounding in my throat!
Tonight, they found me first inside a dream.
Some sexual thing had not gone your way . . .
Your face held nacreous, rotting red and green—
Twists of flesh in, upon it. One eye was
Slipped down within, under that dying mask;
Shone, staring at me—calm hate, misery.
(Poor boy! The other—the non-you, all-you.)
Then that bell came and kissed me in the brain.
And the dragging struck me sore-hearted, then.
Great, shuddering drags! Targeted to goodness,
An arc inside the heart—that broke, grew back,
Broke again. Brief births, draped in flags of blood!
I tried to turn to touch you to wake you.
But could not move. I stirred, screamed—silently.
Then woke. Lights from the canal dawning, dying,
On our walls. I heard the music two branches
Made rubbing on each other. *Then* the bell,
And soon, that long dragging—in the real room.
Go up, go see—if we have a ghost!'

         'No.
I went for you last night. There was nothing.
Dark—and the things I told you.'

        'Darkness—and *things?*'

'Moon enough. Lay your "unpillowed head, fraught with
Sad fears" down, and sleep.'

                              'Tell me last night again.'

'I, in pajamas, in the musk-scented, cold,
Moon-mirroring air. There was nothing there.
Bits of coal glinting bright as broken glass-bits.
(Light riding a hair you hope has not gone white!)
Suitcases put down piled-up—a strange staircase.
A white, white door with one black window stood
In the middle of the mess, leading nowhere.
A big, slightly new photo of the center
Of Paris—that looked all teeth and shadows.
A coat hurled like a headless man on a box.
Scary enough—but only a small chaos,
With that odd, underlying look chaos has,
Of being ordered by its many uses.'

'I'm lonely, I'm lonely because I'm frightened.'

'Listen, to the Old Church bell! The great notes
Drift across the sky . . . echoing their own
Tragic, stately undertone. *Bong . . . bong . . . bong.*
They fill the night.'

'They make me remember
Something cruel—and crude, and sad and funny:
We did not come out to church when they called,
One Sunday on the farm with father, once—
And that night he woke us deep in the night,
So savage and controlled his dog whimpered.
*"All right. Since you were strong enough to cast down
The tower of God today—everybody out,
And lift the northeast corner of the house!"*
We did. My part seemed light. (The weight and pain?
Planning to kill him the rest of the night.)
Stars frozen midway to somewhere, poked their fires . . .
Dark place, unsupportable as an axis
Of shadow. Arms there, of the windmill. Turning
Into the night a fast, false labyrinth.
Sometimes I dream it is what we lifted.'

'What a mad thing—your white-haired dynamo!
"You shall know the truth, and it shall make you me."'

'Poor Pops, I miss his clear-eyed, half-smiling . . .
We must go see him soon. —Ah, come back to bed.
Or, go up! Go see if we have a ghost.
Why sit, staring all-alive out the window?'

'How can one help but be at the window,
Here in your Holland?—Everything's windows.
Unshaded, flowered windows. Darkness slurs them
Now, but before these—big bright boxes showed:
The people and colored objects of life.
Naked windows. Staring sightless, proudly
Oblivious eyes. —A kind of closed openness,
Like the manner you blunt Hollanders have.
Or maybe first, in a wild wet place, windows
Were left uncovered to be a living
Emblem—that held fire, food, family, flowers,
Broke the endlessly folded flat horizon,
And kept out innumerable prying lusts,
Death, dark, cold, and loneliness—'

                              'I like that:
Holland as a flower . . . in the window, sky.'

'Yes, but—down the street in that little, heart-shaped
Section of the city, ladies of the night
Sit—psychedelically-lit—in windows, too.'

'Did you ever have one, of them . . . before me?'

'Once, as I was passing those cubes of fire,
One put her tongue out at me. That little, red,
Original animal, the dance it did—
Seemed to show *me,* my own nakedness! Then
Sank out of sight. Her still white hands, waved me in.
Dying lilts of color in the room. Fishhooks,—
Disapproving uncertainty in her eyes.
Lifts a leg on the bed, letting light pass through
The gauzy, spangled gown. Then dropped it off.
Every body seems its own meaning. Hers?
Purity liking dirty triumph calmly.
Her breasts were so small they seemed shot off, but
Perfecting themselves round at the bottom.
Sucked them. —Grabs my dangling, atavistic fruit—
Crams the pale piece in her mouth. Hear, *feel* her laugh—
Just before I say Oh and it is over.
She shakes her tits free of something, shakes them
Some more. White column, rising. She spits me out
In a sink. Over the bed, burned in English
Into wood, The Golden Rule!'

     'Fine for her,
But not for making love!'

      'Waves, claws of fake fire.
She (not a woman) back in the window.
Bright, dirty banner balked at the labyrinth
Love has entered in.'

    'Paid to love yourself,
Is what it amounts to. Not love, *or* sex!'

'Everyone likes dirty sex. Love loves it.
Another window. —The soul—at separate
Windows sits.'

              'Your soul does!'

                         'It moved, this morning—
Before anything in the world was ghosted.
I loved and needed and wanted and had you.
The sun was the only other face (and force)—
Moving as we moved, looking at us with
What a steady face! Strong, bright softnesses—
Toward, together—a flower! Warmth, depth
Within depth, but flying—with you, offering.
Lights of the leaves far, far-promising . . .'

                              'All
Those strange, round-headed leaves . . .'

                         'You touched me with
The mysterious reach of your branches,
That hold my city up. —Ah, here you are!'

'Do you like me?'

              'Yes . . . kissing, smiling lips.'

'Oh, and I wish it would stop—Thump! Thump! Thump!—
Shot after shot, right into my heart. Go.
See. Be a window, my window. *Shoo it out!*'

'You know old houses make noise, all by themselves.'

'Tell it you're alive, it's dead, and I'm scared.
And that we don't need sensations fluttering
Into us, night after night.'

           'In American,
Or—in my bad Dutch?'

            'Say: *"D'r uit! D'r uit!"*
And it will go. No, *feel* it. It will know
If life is in you, full of angry pride.
But if the poor old thing's so bound to *things*—
(Imagine *being* a sound or a sight,
And desiring to be touched by an object!)
Or, it's socializing it wants—it can stay,
But silence, or out!'

           'Can it do some dusting,
At night?'

           'Yes,—but tell it the house is ours,
Ours for a happy half-year! And the goal
Is not madness! You may even tell it,
The great, kind, fine thing—that we are married,
One month! If it is a good ghost it will go . . .'

'The only good ghost is a dead ghost. Ha.'

'Ha.'

'I'd say—you are the absence of nothing,
Sir. Death. Or—have you ever seen me before,
I'd ask. —Nooooooooooo! (Ghosts never say yes.)
Then how do you know I'm here? (An insult,
To imply you are not there more than he is.)
Flutter, garble, curdle. (Dead or alive,
The Dutch do not have much of the light touch.)
"So"—he'd say,"*Indeed*—" (There was a blow!) Then,
Baring bile-blue chops in a smile of smug,
Self-satisfied inferiority, he'd tell
Me my own joke, word for word, as if his.
(Sung in the ratchet, sprocket sounds of your tongue.)
I: May I ask you a personal question?'

'Me?'

    'No, him— Do you believe in God? *He:*
See here! See here! Do you know who you speak to?
Posthumous Peckelharing, of the fine old firm
Of Wynand Fockink, Amsterdam, XXX—
1632. That's whoooooooo! Then, pointing
Ectoplasmically down at you—*We are not*
Entirely without power, you know—Aha!
I'd say—'

    'No, don't hurt him!'

        'Taking his part, eh?'

'He just wants to come downstairs, like everyone.'

'Aha, I'd say. I see, threatening my wife—'

'He never met a New York wise-guy before.'

'Hoo! See the gulls!'

      'What do they do, these?'

             'What?—
They receive the night and fly, resisting wind.'

'But, *why?* Gulls go inland—sleep on lakes, at night.
My God, something worse keeps crowding in.'

'There is always one atop that flagpole.'

'There is never one atop the flagpole,
Or anywhere else at night!'

      'Look at that
Big one on that great, naked slab of ice,
Floating by in the canal! Stiff, rolling strut.
Gets gawks from others, as if she were their slut.'

'She has a shadow, *and* a reflection . . .'

'They seem to be talking incoherently
To each other—in funny, cat-like screeches.'

'A high, moon-like sound.'

      'There they go!'

46

          'Pieces
Of metal on each other.'

      'Fierce, flying white!
One cries past on outstretched, unmoving wings.'

'An arrow, balked at our window—forever!
(As the arrow goes through the arrow goes through.)'

'They still seem to be there—hovering, headless.
See, the wind making white wings on the water?'

'Yes.'

  'The canal is a calm street of water
Again . . . Trammeled-metal water, pierced by
The spears of the oars of that live green boat.
A great, tattered torch of flowers . . . that glides.
. . . A bright, plastic sack dying up and down . . .
A doll, just afloat. A little bear.'

        'Or—
A dog. See the legs roll under, up, out?'

         'Yes.—
The moon now. The planet that shines at night.'

'Loneliness that makes us all less lonely.'

'And above, almost unnoticed, beyond light
That cold stone has—blue-dark, mirroring small lights,—
Plains of black fire—seeming, but not seeming
Something—an imageless, fierce peacefulness—
The sky.'

    'You seem to say the same thing the strange
Sounds say . . . My heart half-stopped, then beat very,
Very faintly as you spoke. —Feel my heart.'

                     'Yes.'

'Somewhere in those buildings, a gull cries out!
To set wings like white knives to the moon. —No,
To answer your look—I'm not a seagull.'

                   'No . . .'

'They are so old, they are so rickety!
Narrow, tombstone-shaped, silvery-withered,
They look too old to stand, seem too old to fall—
And determined to do either, together!'

'What is the big white top on that building?
Twisted pillars, cloud-bodies, scrolls, seals . . .?'

                    'It is

Amsterdam. I saw it today. It has
Pirates, Justice, God, and Neptune. The weapons
And instruments are painted gold. The rest
Is pigeon-grey, riddled white by pigeon-rain.'

'Are those animals there—blunted, lolling . . .?'

'There are many. The holy horse with one horn.
Cherubs, riding lions. Deep-cut torso bent back,
A bugler blows upon a golden sea-horn!
The angry sea-god pulls him by tight hair down
Into the underside of a wave, which has
Great and shadowed names written in its stone.'

'And God, devouring his own extremities—
On the other side? Or, are they people?'

                                          'S-s-sh!
That is a long, innocent track between
Some eyeless-looking dolphins and the sun . . .
There are angels there—swinging glory-paddles,
Before the one almighty One, it all
Breaks in jagged folds under, advancing.'

                                    'Wow!
Will I wake to find a few dour cupids there,
Suave, sashed lions—because you made it up?'

                                        'No.
Look at the strange cloud with a hole in it . . .'

'Strange to see in a strange country, that giant
Pepsi-Cola bottle-top—stuck up there
Between a spired, distended crown tower-top,
On an open cupola with windows (see,
The stars?) of sky— and that dim, grim, grey, barbed
Phallus.'

49

'That thing looks like (and is called) the
Coal-scuttle, most modern church we have. Supposed
To be a finger, heaven-pointing.'

                                'Pepsi
Peers out, over the city's intricate
Puzzle—smiles his own name red, white, blue—with such
Innocent finality—a faceless gnome.'

'The gnomes here are a political party.'

'Are people here who speak of the good, good?'

'The Gnomes are, or were.'

                        'Hey! The newspaper—
Fell. Fluttering like a divining wing,
Opening. Look at him looking at us! How—?'

'I propped it . . . broken glass. Wind came, knocking.'

'Sent us this standard-bearer of the devil,
In front of the great seal of America—
Winged-Pig, Under Secretary of War!
(See the eagle, spreading its wings behind him?)
His haircut days over, but what hairy wings!
He did not want those things growing from his head.'

'Who would want wings coming out of his head?'

'Or that barbarous, star-studded ball stuck
On a stick into his top! Half-head, all-mouth—
Making a black hole, for all those eggs of war.
In Hell, he would look innocent enough . . .
This sausage-fingered deity points one down
From the others, worms interlocked in a war
For it.—An embryonic ego, in
Cold depths of rage, whose omniphageous, soul-
Altering eyes, punching black holes in the page—
Come out—Just one of those looks could kill you!'

'All that seems stranger than saying: *Nothing is.*'

'And what if the Plutonian powers
Sent him, to show what simple evils we have?
The monkey-eating eagle, America!
It will go through the evolution of
Its own desires, to one last desire, man.'

'As if all of America the Terrible
Could be a doll devils spoke through, from Hell!
What the devil have devils to do with it?
To judge from the photo, this is a man—
(And that's *all* he is) high up in your country,
A glad, eager soldier—leading the vile war.'

'Ugly, self-portrait of the human will!
Oh, what a golden blaze of love and death
Is in that one, self-haunted look Rembrandt has
In his self-portraits! The will is human
Under that lid of light. It pities, marvels!
Put this egg back flat on the floor, face-down.'

'I love you, but we live in a time—a world,
Presently, under dark stripes of force and blood,
Fierce and savage strength for no good purpose.
Death is around, a deepening wound—not ours.
No one can see—moving under moving masks
Of blood, tears bubble and break—lost, faceless eyes.
Suddenly it's fear, all fear to me—us.
Do you have strength—to go with your goodness?'

'Enough to meet your ghost last night.'

                                        'My ghost?'

'Yes.—See? That frilled, gauze-bandage curtain blowing?
Pale, ardent ghost going glittering and
Unconcealed, into an implacable yield
Of blackness.'

                'What ghost?'

                                'That window should be sealed.'

'You pretend to pretend to frighten me more,—
For what I said.'

                        Winds in lancing steel perform.
It was a wind-ghost.'

                        'The ghost! Where was he?'

'He was sitting on a pile of window-frames.
He was sitting *in* a pile of window-frames.'

'You never mentioned any!'

          'See for yourself.'

'No. I'd be dead. What color was he? Tell!'

'Nothing could be more truly the color
Of dead flesh—yellow wax, quicksilver mixed.'

'How is it possible?'

        'I do not know that.'

'Start from the start—go step by step, slowly.'

            'Right.
There *was* a candle—why lie about light?
There was a moon, and the shadow of myself,
And, past any intention of disbelief—
There was a ghost. —Now, now, now!'

          'I'll be still.
—Scared *not* to know!'

       'Went up quickly, angry,
(At you for sending me, *then*) saw those things,
All the masks I told you, plus, one strange thing:
My wedding-ring startled me, in the moonlight . . .
The bright band dimmed. As distance dims, or use.
Then darkened, a cobalt dream of becoming . . .
Gold again. In that desert of moonlight . . .'

'Yes?'

'A sack seemed hung down in back of that white door,
Resting on those frames. *Then*—'

'And *then?*'

'It moved.
Something seemed to move. Something saw me move.
I felt I'd swallowed a piece of the moon.
My bones turned to water. There was a man
Staring at me. Grey around, fading, not grey—'

'—The impact of a ghost, after we made love!'

'Don't get personal.'

'Hah, now—no. Oh, you thing!
But how could you stand there? *Godverdomme!*'

'In *some* way, he was more frightened than me.
White hair spidering around, longer than yours . . .
Twenty years older, but taller, stronger,
Than me—a long man. Eyes, resinous shadow—
But gold! Gold that gave back no gleam. Avid,
Unmoved. So lost in the forces making him.
Then—then . . .'

'What—what?'

'A roll of white paper showed up,
Rolling right into the void of the door.'

'*Nay! Godver—*'

        '—All by itself, out of the room.
He rose. (At the thick edge of terror within
Me, a jolting catch of laughter! He moved
Like this . . . a sort of dapper moral manner—
As if Christ were *treading* water, to music!)
"You're dead, I know you are!" I called. (Word-
Pieces, more than a voice, came out.) Wobbling
Inside the intense, solid whiteness—he glared.
Then, *whoosh!* Metallic green cape rattling behind,
Snarling more to himself than to me: *"He
Smacketh of himself—surely justice and
Mercy will follow!"* Some bible-babble,
Mixed with an odd paranoiac pep, and rage.
Before he reached me, he—like a round drop
Of rain rolling on glass—widened, and was gone.
Lovely light unbiddable steps vanishing.
As over water. My candle out, dark. So.'

'I never would have dared to go to sleep.
A ghost!'

      'A real, live ghost.'

            '*Green cape rattling . . .?*'

'Yes, we have a loony in the attic.
But I liked him . . . his noble self-pity.'

'Where is he now? No! I'll be still. I'm ashamed.
Do you like me?'

'Yes. Like you?—I *am* you.'

'Oh.'

'You have the beautiful, dwindling, visionary,
Face of a cat.'

'O, me alone!'

'But why
Do you yawn your mouth back flat and wide like that—
More baby than cat? Frowning, helpless to cry.
A face grimacing at its own grimace.'

'Big man scared me, statue.—Clock, an eye.'

'What?'

'*The dog it was that died.* I loved him . . . so.'

'You loom past me, so unsatisfied and strange . . .'

'My shores beset by thousand secret spires,
The heart must go by air—but flutters, lost.'

'Your eyes are open, but you are asleep!'

'The momentary black shutter, opening.
Infinities keep crowding in. I see.
The eye shrouds smaller, flowering yellow
Demonic gleams.'

'I must stop this, now. Hey!'

'The little, baby-tree, grown halfway up,
Slant out of the dark round tree. Ah, and there!
Bird-head in the beak of a flying bird!
The sky and hill is darkened. I must stay—'

'*Dear*. I'm afraid to touch her, to move her.'

'I must stay, and wait for the fire-bodies.
My God, trust Samson to put fire in there,
Into the immemorial juncture, sex!
As he put himself in-between the pillars.
Foxes have to have live fire up in them—
Flower-faced foxes!'

                    'That passage her father
Read at the wedding! But—the firebrands were tied
In their tails, in the tails tied together.'

'Hundreds, into the enemy harvest!'

'The enemy—who? That giant baby. *Fink*.
To read Samson, at a wedding! Now, she—'

'All angry muscle under his unharmed hair,
I hear him talk to a talking tower—God.'

'Sick-white in her face, eyes longing, with pain . . .
Oh, she believed in my ghost, more than I!'

'*God:* Stick torches in them! Sticks red with fire, blood.
To make a running signal on the plain.
In vines and wheat, bright as maidens when they wed.
Samson: How, Sir? *God:* Foxes have their holes.
Samson: Stinks of former food there. Satan's flag.
God: Ha. *Samson:* How many must I, O Lord?
God: Many as can feed the wind, or your love
Of me. But do not believe I believe
In material brightness, or by strange honors
Am inciting devils to love me, God.
Samson: O, no. *God:* World scans that way, now:
"Plain danger . . . bombs, pondering limitless
Global war . . . moved, but not destroyed. Tied his hands.
Million-man American withdrawal-bombing.
Bombing thee—no, bombing *three* countries, and
Invading two—in order to evacuate
One. So-called misunderstanding-bombing.
Mounting belief . . . peace . . . owes . . . Nixon." The devil
Hath rhetoric to maintain himself by—
Has he not, Samson? *Samson:* None save himself,
Lord. *God:* Good. But—time loses time. Go now.
Fire them there like the red salamander!
(Whose rapturous costume, soon you must wear.)'

'She snapped that newspaper down like a snake.
O, she believed in my ghost more than me!'

'*Samson:* Sir, you know better things—but I
Would enloin the apterous insect. *God:*
Such words teach the devil how to revel.
Samson: But *Blackhat* is winning everything.
Saracens shrewing at Solomon's seal!
Song-birds, asleep on sinistrous service-trees!
Sifacas—a-playing in hibiscus! *God:*
O, Samson. A horn has a noise, but can it
Whisper in the ear of a scorpion?
Wait and you will see, what I do with him.'

'How her voice is a . . . brave, small-creatured cry!'

'The single erect, or arching stem, bears
Ovate, or lance-shaped, sharp-pointed sessile leaves
In the exils of which appear narrow
Greenish, whitish or pinkish bell-shaped flowers,
Or slender, drooping stalks, followed by berries,
Globular, pulpy, usually bluish.'

                    'Wow!
That sounds like sex with three x's! But how dies—
Does the dictionary come in here? She—*she.*'

'The plant springs from a fleshy, creeping rootstock—
Scars of last year's shoots leave strange, seal-like marks—'

'Solomon's seal! Unaccountable stain. *Two.*'

'Here they come! Many. *Many.* Samson's signal.
Their rich, red hides heave yellow gowns of fire.
Their eyes are squeezed shut, in ecstatic slits
Of pain. This is the fox who knows his grace.
Black selves stem open like umbrellas, crowd
Into a cloud of violence.'

                    'I must stop her!'

'The umbilicus comes cobraing out,
Forms a giant pillar of purple fire,
Shooting upward at tremendous speed. The top
(Many masks grimacing, living totem)
Struggling to be free, a creature—it breaks off.
Floating upward, momentum carrying
It to the height of heaven. Another!
The decapitated monster grows a new head,
While the first one floats off into the blue—
A flower-form, gigantic petals curving
Downward. Creamy-white outside, red inside.'

'Moving around me now . . . a restless hostage.'

'That cloud caught fire from the fire-tortured foxes!
Lights adrift without a world, we are—love is.
A wide, dirty ledge is our present reserve.
Today, I want some tulips, or some daffodils.
Trumpet-daffodils, trumpeting of Spring!
Isn't it a miracle, we're together?'

'Remember who you are! Who are you?'

                              'Your wife—
Me.'

   'Hah! Oh, fine. I love that. I love you.'

'Hello. Dear. How funny to be frightened.
How funny to be frightened in Holland,
In an old house, like a big drum! Suppose
A ghost still is beating in here? So long as
Not in the heart, or our city.—Say my name.'

About the Author

RAPHAEL RUDNIK is a native New Yorker, born in 1933. After graduating Bard College, he worked at a variety of jobs, including: publicity writer, social investigator, proofreader, gambler, and College English teacher, and took his M.A. at Columbia. He has been a Guggenheim Fellow, and was chosen by Robert Lowell, John Berryman and M. L. Rosenthal for the first Delmore Schwartz Memorial Poetry Award. Mr. Rudnik has lived in Holland during the past few years.